Original title:
Snowflakes and Silent Dreams

Copyright © 2024 Creative Arts Management OÜ
All rights reserved.

Author: Benjamin Caldwell
ISBN HARDBACK: 978-9916-94-618-3
ISBN PAPERBACK: 978-9916-94-619-0

Enchanted Chill

In winter's grip, we all do laugh,
With frosty breath, we share our gaff.
The world turns white, a snowy cloak,
We slip and slide, it's just a joke.

Hot cocoa spills on coats so bright,
As children giggle at the sight.
The snowman falls, a comical mess,
In this chill, we feel so blessed.

Skyward Drift

Up in the air, a flurry flies,
I catch a cold one—what a surprise!
With every snowball, a playful fight,
Laughter echoes all through the night.

A snowy hat atop my mate,
He looks like quite the chilly state!
We roll and tumble without a care,
In this frosty fun, we all can share.

Snowbound Stories

Bundled snug like sausages,
We scheme and plot with laughter's fizz.
Tales of sledding, oh what a ride,
We tumble down the slopes with pride.

Our noses red, our spirits high,
As friends we laugh, the time flies by.
With hot pie warmth and silly games,
We celebrate each other's names.

Frostbitten Whispers

Frosty whispers float through the night,
With goofy grins, we feel alright.
As hot cakes flip and syrup spills,
Our merry moments give us thrills.

In hats too big, we try to run,
Chasing each other—oh, what fun!
Ice angels made with flapping arms,
We can't resist their frosty charms.

Silent Heartbeats in Snow

In winter's chill, we slide and sway,
Our mittens flop, hip-hip-hooray!
Snowmen stumble, hats askew,
Just like us, when snowballs flew.

We race on down, the slopes all bright,
Giggling loud, such pure delight!
Frosty faces, noses red,
Can't catch breath; oh, what was said?

Celestial Crystals

Tiny wonders from the sky,
Catch them quick, and watch 'em fly!
They dance like bees, oh so spry,
But melt away; oh my, oh my!

Laughter echoes through the freeze,
As bundled friends just aim to please.
We toss and tumble, squeals ignite,
While icy kicks make spirits light.

The Hush of Winter Nights

The moon peeks out, a silver cheek,
Of snowball fights, we hardly speak.
But brewing cocoa fills the air,
With marshmallows tossed, oh what a flair!

Under stars, we twirl and spin,
"Oh no! My hat just flew off, grin!"
Chasing it, we trip and fall,
Laughter echoes, catching all.

Frozen Meadow Reveries

In fields of white, where we play coy,
We build a fort, oh what a joy!
But wait! A snowball thieves our game,
"Who threw that?!" we shout in claim!

With giggles bright, we plot and plan,
To sneak and launch our snowy span.
Through chilly air, our tempers rise,
Yet joy remains in each surprise.

The Gentle Touch of Hibernation

In winter's grip, the creatures snooze,
They dream of cheese, or maybe shoes.
A bear rolls over, makes a fluff,
While birds just hope there's not enough.

The frogs are snug, all lost in thought,
Their winter home, a cozy spot.
A mouse writes tales of daring feats,
Whilst nibbling crumbs and winter treats.

The world outside, a frosty chill,
Yet here indoors, it's warm and still.
As visions dance in slumber's clutch,
We giggle softly at the gentle touch.

A Symphony in White

A winter breeze plays a funny song,
As icicles dance and jive along.
The trees all sway with snowy hats,
While rabbits plot their acrobatic spats.

A snowman sports a scarf so bright,
He chuckles as he "sings" at night.
The flakes cocoon each twinkling light,
Behold the sight, a pure delight!

The squirrels slide, they laugh and leap,
Sliding down the slopes so steep.
The world is loud, but with such grace,
Winter's tune puts smiles on each face.

Ethereal Echoes in the Stillness

In twilight's hush, the whispers clear,
Of giggles lost in winter cheer.
A sprite on skates, so deft and spry,
Spins tales of how the owls fly high.

A polar bear tries on a hat,
But oh dear me, he's quite too fat!
He wobbles here, and tumbles there,
While giggling geese offer a stare.

Under stars that blink and shine,
We tiptoe through the frozen line.
With memories that prompt a quip,
We weave joy from the frosty slip.

Twinkling Moments in the Quiet

As snow drapes softly on the ground,
A pair of mittens can be found.
One's missing, no one's quite aware,
An ice-bound sock? Oh, what a pair!

The moonlight winks, a cheeky friend,
It teases trees that twist and bend.
A noodle cat meows "I want heat!"
While dreaming of that noodle treat.

In silence rich, the secrets flow,
As winter wraps us soft and slow.
With laughter floating on the breeze,
We find the truth in frosty freeze.

Celestial Drifts

Float like a feather, fall like a star,
I built a snowman who's now a bizarre.
His carrot nose wiggled, just like a worm,
He sneezed a big sneeze, it sent him a-turn!

Twirl through the air, I lost my last sock,
My snowmen are missing, they're out for a walk!
A dance-off with rooftops, what a sight to behold,
I giggle and slip, as the stories unfold.

Tranquility in Silence

The chill in the air, a soft tittering sound,
My house cat is plotting, with mischief unbound.
She leaps off the couch like a flash in the night,
Landing in snow, oh what a silly sight!

With mittens on hands and scarf like a clown,
I tripped on a snowdrift and fell on my gown.
The world starts to chuckle; I rise with some flair,
In my frosted white kingdom, I tumble and share.

The Art of Letting Go

I once made a snowball, it flew high and wide,
It hit Uncle Fred—who started to glide!
He spun like a top, then slipped on his rear,
While muttering something, all fuzzy and clear.

With cheeks rosy red, he chuckled out loud,
I asked if he'd dance, and he joined the snow crowd.
The snow might be cold, but our laughter's a blaze,
As we twirl through the flurries, lost in a daze.

Caught in a Wintry Dream

My sled has a mind of its own - such a tease,
It rolls down the hill with the greatest of ease.
I held on for dear life, just squeals and some shrieks,
Down we went tumbling, like two clumsy freaks.

The air filled with giggles, joy twinkled bright,
As I found myself caught in a snowball fight.
With laughter like bells, we played until night,
In this whimsical whirlwind, everything feels right.

Icy Reveries

Tiny dancers swirl and twirl,
Facing chilly winds they whirl,
They land upon my nose and laugh,
In this winter's quirky path.

Frosty whispers in the breeze,
Tickling cheeks with icy tease,
They giggle as they pile up high,
A snowy mountain in my eye.

Each leap and skip, a frosty jest,
Ready for a snowball fest,
Laughter echoes all around,
In this winter's magic found.

With every plop and gentle kiss,
They turn my frown into pure bliss,
Painting scenes of giggly cheer,
As winter's jokes draw ever near.

The Quiet of Falling White

A gentle hush upon the street,
As winter weaves her cozy sheet,
In their frosty waltz they glide,
Chasing dreams with giggles wide.

Wandering through the chilly air,
My boots crunch carefully with care,
A snowman wobbles, tipsy gaze,
In this merry, icy maze.

Hot cocoa waits with marshmallow crowns,
As laughter dances round the towns,
Each sip we take, a warm embrace,
As frosty fun fills every space.

The world's a stage for chilly plays,
With frozen antics, woozy ways,
In this stillness, giggles bloom,
As winter's spirit finds its room.

Veils of Crystal Light

The world is draped in dazzling white,
Turning simple paths to flight,
Sleds race down with squeals of glee,
While fluffy clouds play hide and see.

Icicles dangle, sharp and grand,
Like winter's wand in frosty hand,
They catch the light, oh what a show,
As frosty fairies dance below.

A snowball fight breaks out in jest,
With friendly hits, we give our best,
Laughter erupts, a joyful sound,
As winter's fun spins all around.

With every flake, a jolly cheer,
As frozen funtime draws us near,
The magic stirs with every sight,
In this wonderland of crisp delight.

Touched by Frost

A sprinkle here, a dot right there,
The world transformed with icy flair,
Each footstep leaves a fleeting trace,
   Chasing marvels in this place.

The trees wear coats of shimmering white,
   A sparkly crown, a pure delight,
They sway and dance in frosty glee,
   Whispering secrets just for me.

A chubby squirrel, quite bemused,
Fumbles on the ice, so confused,
He wobbles, tumbles, what a sight,
   In this oddball winter light.

Laughter rings in the frozen air,
As chilly antics become our care,
This frosty humor all around,
In every flake, happiness found.

The Calm Before Winter's Flight

In the hush where whispers roam,
A penguin slips, he's far from home.
With a waddle and a flurry,
He plans his icy, snowy curry.

Mittens dance like tiny feet,
While snowmen try to stay discreet.
A squirrel dons a fluffy hat,
And laughs at all the silly cats.

The moon peeks through a velvet haze,
While shadows play a chilly maze.
A bunny hops, but trips and flips,
Into a pile of frosty slips.

So cheers to winter and its charm,
With giggles wrapped in cozy warm.
Where every slip and playful fall,
Turns into laughter, oh, for all!

Veils of Frost and Midnight Dreams

As icicles dangle like long beards,
A ladybug sneezes, it's one for the years.
She covers her nose with a tiny glove,
Laughing at snowflakes that dance above.

The deer in the woods have started a band,
With a drummer who's cheerful and made of sand.
The melodies freeze - oh what a sight!
As they sway joyfully in pale moonlight.

Ice skaters twirl but land in a heap,
All giggles and snow, with friends in a sweep.
Frosty the snowman gives them a wave,
While plotting a dance, he hopes to be brave.

At night snow shines, it's quite a tease,
But down in the trees, there's an old wise bee.
He chuckles and buzzes in frigid delight,
What a silly, snowy winter night!

The Stillness of Crystal Wishes

In a field where wishes glide and slide,
Pigeons wear scarves and strut with pride.
A rabbit makes a snow-cake treat,
While squirrels gather nuts with dances neat.

The stars above play peek-a-boo,
As moles in the ground complain of the blue.
With flicks of tails, and twirls galore,
They ensure the night's never a bore.

A fox with flair puts on a show,
With flips and spins all in the snow.
But oh! He slips and goes for a ride,
Launching ashore, with no fear, no pride.

So gather your friends, let's all come play,
In a world where laughter leads the way.
With stars and wonders wrapped in white,
Making memories, oh what a delightful sight!

A Quiet Reverie in the Snowy Twilight

Under the trees, the whispers creep,
While kittens roll in their cozy heap.
Chasing snowflakes, they tumble and dive,
Creating a ruckus, oh how they strive!

Bears in pajamas take a long stroll,
Pausing to giggle, they're on a roll.
Talking to owls who hoot with glee,
It's bedtime for magic, can't you see?

The moon laughs softly, casting its light,
As critters play hide and seek in the night.
A hedgehog sighs, "Oh what a thrill,
To frolic in snow at such a chill!"

So let's twirl around in the frosty air,
With giggles and grins we all want to share.
In this snowy wonderland so bright,
Humor dances merrily, oh what a sight!

Threads of Ice

Tiny twirls dance down so nice,
They land on noses, oh what a price!
With laughter bright beneath the trees,
We sidestep puddles like clumsy bees.

Boots are stuck, we're stuck in place,
I break the ice with a silly face.
The wind is chuckling, I'm in a spin,
Who knew a cold day could feel like a win?

A hat too big, framing my grin,
I chase the fluff as it twirls in the wind.
Wishing on fluff like a silly old fool,
It lands on my head—now I look like a tool!

Giggles echo where snowmen stand,
With carrot noses and twiggy hands.
The chilly air fills with laughter's sound,
In this frosty chaos, fun is found.

A Pint of Stillness

In the stillness, we shake and quake,
Noses red like a ripe fruit cake.
We sit with mugs that steam and swirl,
Warming our fingers with a cozy twirl.

The foam on top dances and plays,
Like kittens on ice in delicate sprays.
Each sip is a giggle, a chuckle, a cheer,
Our warmth wraps around, just like a blanket here.

In a world of white, our laughter's the sound,
As we slip and slide, not making a sound.
With each little tumble, a symphony of glee,
Who knew hot chocolate could set our hearts free?

So here's to the moments, the slips, and the spills,
To frosty mischief and all of the thrills.
While pints stay still, our spirits take flight,
In the gentle embrace of a sweet, snowy night.

Where Shadows Curl

Where shadows curl, mischief does reign,
As snow drifts whisper on the windowpane.
A snowball fight, oh what a delight,
Like kids on sugar, we laugh with all our might.

On frosted grass, we dash and chase,
With a slip and a slide, we embrace the race.
Laughter tumbles like beads on a string,
In this chilly hide-and-seek, joy takes wing.

The sun plays peekaboo from behind the clouds,
Drawing silly shapes and giggling crowds.
We dance with shadows, our antics unfold,
With a frosty giggle, new memories are told.

Snowmen wobble, hats askew,
We clink our mugs, "To nonsense, woo-hoo!"
In the magic of frosty light we find,
That silliness can warm the coldest mind.

Frosted Mornings

Frosted mornings, what a sight!
With noses pink and cheeks so bright.
We tumble out, all bundled tight,
Turning simple steps into a wild flight.

Chasing dog tails and fluffs of white,
Joking 'bout maps, navigator's plight.
We spin and twirl, oh what a show,
As snowflakes pirouette, putting on a glow.

In mismatched mittens, we gather 'round,
Making the softest, silliest sounds.
With laughter ringing through the air,
Each frosty moment, we dance with care.

Through frozen frames, our smiles freeze,
Yet in our hearts, joy never flees.
So here's to mornings wrapped in fun,
Where winter's game is never done.

Echoes of a Frozen Silence

In winter's grip, the world turns white,
A snowman sneezes, what a sight!
With carrot nose and arms askew,
He waves goodbye; he's off to brew.

The trees wear coats all fluffy and round,
While squirrels in hats make silly sounds.
A penguin slide, let's have some fun,
The chilly air makes everyone run!

Icicles dangle like toothy grins,
While snowballs fly; oh where's my skin?
We build a fort, then shout, "We're kings!"
And dance like fools as laughter springs.

So here we are, in laughter's thrall,
In this white wonderland, we'll have a ball.
With frosty cheeks and hearts so bright,
We'll cherish the joy of this merry night.

Glistening Wishes on Winter's Canvas

A frosty canvas, pure and grand,
We doodle hearts with our mittened hand.
The ground is soft, a gentle bed,
Where turtles tip-toe, they'll hit their head!

With cocoa mugs and marshmallows galore,
We sip and giggle, then spill on the floor.
The cocoa's hot, but our lips are cold,
We share silly tales, just like we're old.

Chasing each other in a giggly spree,
A snowball flies, oh what a spree!
Laughter echoes as we tumble down,
In this frosty realm, we wear the crown.

So let the flakes swirl in whimsical flight,
As we dream and play deep into the night.
The magic here is a silly tease,
In this winter wonderland, we do as we please!

The Chill of Serene Enchantment

In the chill, socks dance on the floor,
With frosty toes, who could ask for more?
A cat in boots tries to sneak by,
But lands in a pile—oh, me oh my!

The air is crisp, with laughter's breath,
We plot a heist of snow to bequeath.
A snowball bandit with a wink so sly,
Steals my hat; oh, that cheeky guy!

We race the wind on our rubber sleds,
While giggles escape from our frozen heads.
A snowman's grin, he throws back his hat,
"Why don't you try?" "Hey, don't chat with that!"

With whispers sweet and frosty glee,
We craft our dreams in giddy spree.
The chill ignites a spark so bright,
In this whimsical dance, we take flight!

Traces of Ethereal Beauty

With every flake, a giggle falls,
I wear my boots like winter's calls.
The world is a canvas, playful and bright,
Where penguins waddle in pure delight.

Mittens tossed, a snowball fight,
The laughter rings, oh what a sight!
A hamster in frost holds court today,
As we cheer and frolic, hip-hip-hooray!

Through frozen trees, a sneak attack,
A plump little bunny with a fuzzy back.
He hops away with a burst of cheer,
While we giggle loud, the fun is near.

At dusk, we sing serenades so sweet,
Wishing for ice cream—we can't be beat!
With magic in our hearts, we prance and sway,
In this enchanted realm, we play all day.

Frosted Retreat

In winter's chill, we bundle tight,
With scarves that dance, a silly sight.
Hot cocoa spills upon our toes,
We laugh and slip on ice like pros.

The snowman's grin, a frosty cheek,
Listens to secrets we softly speak.
Our mittens fight, a snowball clash,
Each throw a giggle, a silly splash.

Now frozen toes, we hop away,
From snowmen that beg us to stay.
With every slip, we cheer our fate,
In our frosted retreat, it's never too late!

We toss the flakes, we'd give a cheer,
For winter days, we hold so dear.
As nightfall whispers, we dance in glee,
In a land where joy is always free.

An Odyssey of Icy Silence

In the quiet frost, we roam with grace,
Ice-crunching sounds, a thrilling chase.
A penguin waddle, we imitate,
While giggling softly, it feels just great.

A sled of dreams, we race down hills,
With breathless laughs and silly thrills.
The frozen air, it tickles our nose,
Like snowflakes jumping, nobody knows.

Hot soup awaits, but we can't resist,
A snowball fight? Oh, we can't miss!
Each toss a laugh, each throw a toast,
In this icy saga, we share the most.

Oh the fun of falls, the joy in the freeze,
With giddy hearts, we dance with ease.
In stillness found, our spirits take flight,
In our odyssey, everything feels right.

Gift of the Frozen Night

Beneath the stars, the world is bright,
With icy gifts wrapped up in white.
We twirl around like dizzy sprites,
In a frozen wonder, full of delights.

Our noses red, we sip and giggle,
In this frosty trance, we twist and wiggle.
The moon then winks, a cheeky sprite,
As snowflakes join our snowy night.

A snowman dressed in holiday flair,
With a carrot nose, who's staving off despair.
Together we cheer, a joyous sight,
On this chilly adventure, all feels right.

The laughter rings, we spin and shout,
In frozen jokes, there's never a doubt.
These are our treasures of pure delight,
In the gift of evenings wrapped up tight.

Where Frost Meets Dreams

In a winter's tale, where giggles blend,
With frosty wishes that never end.
A snowcat prances, all furry and sly,
Chasing the flakes that dance in the sky.

With fluffy hats, we strut about,
In our ice palace, we spin and shout.
A penguin parade, everyone sings,
To laughter and joy, the cheer it brings!

The chill doesn't stop our wild whims,
We toss out snowballs, we swing our limbs.
Each little slip brings shrieks of surprise,
In this frosty wonderland, laughter flies!

So here we twirl, in our love for the freeze,
Where dreams take flight with the greatest of ease.
In this frosty land, we chase the gleam,
Where what's most absurd becomes our dream.

The Dance of Frost

Tiny twirls on a chilly breeze,
They spin and skip, oh what a tease!
A frosty ballet on rooftops high,
With pirouettes that almost fly.

They twinkle down on unsuspecting heads,
Causing giggles instead of dreads.
A snowball fight breaks out in glee,
Where laughter echoes, wild and free.

The icicles laugh, hanging with flair,
While snowmen waltz without a care.
A playful flurry, a whimsical sight,
As winter dances into the night.

Each chilly gust tells a joke in flight,
In this frosty world, all feels just right.
So grab your mittens and join the fun,
In the dance of frost, we're never done!

Shimmering Hush

A quiet hush blankets the ground,
Where mischief hides all around.
Whispers of giggles in the air,
As pranks unfold without a care.

The trees wear coats of sparkling white,
Playful shadows dart out of sight.
A frosty wink from the moonlit glow,
Silly secrets that only snow knows.

Frogs in hats and dogs on sleds,
Make the world spin on its heads.
Dancing through drifts with style and flair,
Each frosty moment past thin air.

Why be quiet when life's so grand?
Snowball laughter across the land.
In this shimmering pause, we find,
The joy of folly intertwined!

Illusions in Ice

Mirrors of ice reflecting the fun,
With silly shapes under the sun.
A hopscotch game where all the rules,
Are written by winter's playful fools.

The frozen pond becomes a stage,
Kids rush out, releasing their rage.
A slip and slide turns into a dance,
Wonders abound, no second chance.

Bunnies in scarves prancing about,
In laughter, there's hardly a doubt.
Slapstick skids and tumbling falls,
Each chilly laugh bounces off walls.

With illusions formed under soft skies,
We find our joy in each other's eyes.
In this frozen land, the heart beats bright,
As we chase our dreams in the shimmering light!

Snowbound Whispers

Hush now, hear the secrets being told,
Of frosty adventures, brave and bold.
A whisper here, a lookout there,
In every nook, fun's everywhere.

Sleds coast down with giggles and screams,
Pouring disbelief into sweet dreams.
A snowman's hat that slyly asks,
For a carrot nose, the perfect task!

Each flake that lands brings a cue,
To silly games and pranks anew.
With snowball cheers filling the ache,
In the warmth of laughter, we awake.

As moonlight dances on drifts of white,
We twirl in the joy of this merry night.
So let's embrace the wonders we find,
In snowbound whispers that tease the mind!

Frosted Petals on a Gentle Wind

Tiny bits of fluff drift down,
Floating softly without a frown.
They tickle noses, what a tease,
Like dancing fairies in the breeze.

A cat leaps high, a comical sight,
Chasing dreams of airborne delight.
It lands in a pile, what a mess,
Covered in white, can't quite confess!

Children laugh with gleeful shouts,
As fluffy wonders turn to flouts.
Their mittens soaked, a soggy bliss,
Building castles, oh, what a kiss!

Giggles echo, their cheeks like rose,
In this frozen jest, everyone knows.
Cocoa warms hands from chilly fun,
With stories and laughter, they can't be done!

The Quiet Lullaby of Winter

Whispers brush the sleeping ground,
In a world where giggles abound.
Cats in coats that look absurd,
Hiding from what they've never heard.

Puppies prance with wagging tails,
Chasing shadows on the trails.
A snowman winks, it sure could talk,
With carrot nose and twig-like stock.

Hot soup spills, a saucy plight,
A feast of warmth through chilly night.
In dance of bread and creamy brew,
Laughter drifts, old stories too.

Under skies of lace and twirl,
Joy rides high in a playful swirl.
An age-old tale made fresh again,
As snowflakes settle like silly friends!

Veils of Ice Beneath the Stars

Glittering jewels on branches play,
They look like tricksters in ballet.
Each leaf a surprise, each glint a jest,
Nature's Gams in a winter fest.

Frosty breath creates a fog,
Hide and seek with the dog.
What's that twinkle? Oh, a sleigh,
Dashing through in a cheeky way!

The moon's a joker, glowing bright,
Winking down with a frosty light.
In night's embrace, the stories grow,
Of sneaky snowmen and hats thrown low.

From frosty cheeks to joyful sighs,
The night is full of surprise highs.
With laughter ringing through the night,
Beneath the stars, it all feels right!

Celestial Patterns on a Frozen Night

Patterns swirl in chilly air,
Whirls and twirls, who knows where?
Like quilted dreams across a field,
A tapestry waiting to be revealed.

Fingers cold, a nose bright red,
Skipping through with laughter spread.
Equation of fun in winter's mix,
Bouncing about like silly tricks.

Hot cider spills; oh, what a scene,
Floating marshmallows, a sugary sheen.
A lighthearted jibe at winter's reign,
In every sip, a giggle gain.

As stars burst forth in sparkly cheer,
What a magic time of year!
With every giggle and each warm hug,
These chilly nights all go snug!

The Soul's Winter Pause

In winter's chill, we find our fun,
With mittens on, we start to run.
The snowman waits, with eyes of coal,
His carrot nose, a funny goal.

We slip and slide, it's quite the sight,
As laughter echoes through the night.
A friendly snowball flies on by,
Oh dear! That wasn't meant to fly!

On sleds we race, like birds in flight,
Each twist and turn brings sheer delight.
With frozen feet and rosy cheeks,
We dance and prance, the joy peaks.

So here we sit, in frosty glee,
With icy treats, both wild and free.
A moment's pause, we share a grin,
In winter's grasp, let the fun begin!

Frozen Reflections

The world is dressed in white attire,
While laughter crackles like a fire.
We stumble on the slickest lanes,
And giggle as the chaos reigns.

The frosty air tickles our noses,
As playful winds pull funny poses.
With every plop, a winter splash,
We dive into the chilly crash.

The puddles freeze in silly shapes,
A bear, a bike, and jumping apes!
We take a photo, quick and sly,
And flip it into the sky.

With frozen laughs and silly grins,
We cherish moments, where joy begins.
In this frosted world, we find delight,
Reflecting fun in purest white.

Gentle Winter Night

The moonlight glimmers on the snow,
As cuddly critters put on a show.
A squirrel slips, a raccoon rolls,
In winter's play, they stretch their souls.

The stars peep down with winks and giggles,
While frosty grounds send up little jiggles.
A snowball fight on the garden path,
Who knew winter could spark such wrath?

Hot cocoa warms our frozen hearts,
With marshmallows floating, joy imparts.
We sip in rhythm, with laughter's beat,
As snowflakes swirl and dance on feet.

And as we share this chilly night,
We find in fun, pure delight.
With every giggle, a moment sewn,
In gentle warmth, we're never alone.

Elusive Frosting Dreams

In the icy realm of white delight,
Where wishes twinkle with purest light.
A snowman sings with a silly voice,
As we all gather, it's our choice.

The cupcakes freeze with frosting bright,
In dreams of laughter, what a sight!
A cherry on top, or maybe three,
As we build our sweet jubilee.

The flakes fall soft, like whispers clear,
Each one a giggle, bringing cheer.
And chasing dreams through winter's maze,
We twirl in joy, in the frosty haze.

So let's embrace this wacky scene,
Where every moment feels like a dream.
With icy fun and hearty laughs,
In this magical frost, the spirit crafts.

Whispers of Winter's Veil

Tiny dancers fall from skies,
Landing softly like surprise.
They tickle noses, jackets too,
Creating giggles, just for you.

Snowmen grinning, carrot noses,
Dance around in funny poses.
The dog leaps high, he takes a bite,
Then rolls in piles with pure delight.

As squirrels skate on branches bare,
They tumble down without a care.
The world is wrapped in fluffy white,
While we warm hands and laugh each night.

Hot cocoa spills; we can't resist,
With marshmallows that twist and twist.
Each sip a chuckle in the cold,
While winter tales are sweetly told.

Crystal Echoes

A shiny world where laughter glows,
As icy breath makes funny shows.
The trees wear coats with sparkling sheen,
Nature's joke on the winter scene.

Chasing flakes that tumble down,
We trip and slip with comical frown.
But laughter erupts when we collide,
With snowball fights that won't subside.

Cheerful snowmen steal the show,
With goofy hats and round, bright glow.
They wave their arms, a frosty cheer,
As kids scream joy when sledding near.

And while we shiver, hearts are warm,
In every flurry, there's a charm.
Winter's canvas, a playful sight,
Where giggles dance on winter's night.

Frosted Fantasies

The chilly air brings silly visages,
As snowflakes wear their funny disguises.
A rabbit slipping, loses its hat,
While penguins waddle, where are they at?

The snowman toasts with a mug near,
Shouting cheers with frosted cheer.
With fuzzy scarves and pie to share,
We celebrate moments without a care.

Each sparkle on the ground we trace,
Turns our frowns to a silly face.
As we twirl in piles of cotton white,
Winter's joy makes everything bright.

As the moon giggles, casting beams,
We dance along outlandish dreams.
A whimsical world, where laughter stays,
In every flake that comes to play.

Dreamscapes of Chill

A wonderland of frosty glee,
With cotton clouds for you and me.
We chase quick shadows, soft and light,
In fuzzy boots that fit just right.

The frozen pond's a comic stage,
As ducks slide by, they act like sage.
With flippers flapping, they take a fall,
And laughter echoes through it all.

Fluffy creatures bounce and spin,
In winter's game, let's not give in.
A snowball here, a tumble there,
We giggle loudly through the air.

Though chilly winds may make us squeal,
In this dreamscape, fun is real.
With every breath and icy cheer,
Winter's laughter brings us near.

Night's Whispering Chill

In the night, the chill may tease,
Biting air with stealthy ease.
I wore my hat, two scarves, it's true,
Yet still, my ears turned blue.

A snowman winks, he's quite a pro,
With button eyes all in a row.
He cracks a joke about the freeze,
While I stumble in mismatched knees.

The moonlight beams, a spotlight show,
While penguins dance in lines, you know?
They slip and slide, with flair and grace,
I trip, but laugh, can't win this race.

A flurry swirls, the world's a blur,
I try to catch it, oh what a stir!
With every plop, my head I shake,
Why's winter fair play a funny mistake?

Frozen Thoughts

Chilling thoughts take icy flight,
As I sip cocoa, oh what a sight!
Marshmallows bounce like tiny dreams,
In my cup, life's silly themes.

The snowbanks grow, a joyful heap,
While kids create, the laughter's deep.
Their snowball wars, what a delight,
But here I stand, caught in mid-flight.

With mittens on, I can't hold tight,
As a snowball comes, oh what a fright!
I duck and weave, but miss the aim,
Laughter rings out, I'm not to blame.

The evening falls, the world aglow,
Neighbors argue who's the best in dough.
As cookies crumble and frosting spills,
Winter's magic gives me the chills.

Dreaming in White

In a blanket of fluff, I drift and sway,
Wrapped up tight, I wish you'd stay.
A pillow fight with feathery friends,
   All out giggles as chaos blends.

I roll and tumble, what a snowball,
Each twist and turn, I try not to fall.
The dogs play tag, they run with glee,
While I stash my snacks, in case they see.

I build a fort, a throne so grand,
Just a little shy of being bland.
With marshmallow shields, I'm ready for war,
Against the fluff that lands at my door.

But in sweet dreams, I swiftly sail,
On candy canes and ginger ale.
With giggles and whispers, high above,
This frosty place, I simply love.

A Canvas of Silence

A quiet hush blankets the way,
As frosty fingers start to play.
The world painted pure, a frosty sheet,
While my hot cocoa all stays neat.

Tiny critters, with furry paws,
Squeak and slide, then pause with guffaws.
Snowflakes drift like silly jokes,
While I perform for flurry folks.

Each step I take, a crunch and crack,
Drawing laughter that won't hold back.
With every slip, I twist and twirl,
I toss my hat; oh, here we whirl!

So gather round, let laughter ring,
In this winter, let merriment spring.
We're not too serious, it's all in fun,
In this quiet space, we've all but won.

Shimmering Secrets in the Chill

In the frosty air, a rumor flies,
A snowman with googly eyes!
He dances with joy on winter's stage,
While penguins ponder, should they engage?

There's laughter in each swirling flake,
As squirrels prank, for fun's own sake.
A tumble here, a slip and slide,
It's a merry mess they can't abide!

With scarves that twirl and hats that sway,
They spin and twirl, what a grand ballet!
Each gust of wind a chuckling breeze,
As they fall down, oh, what a tease!

Let's build a critter for a laugh,
A chicken or cat, made of winter craft.
As laughter warms the chilly night,
Their giggles shine with pure delight!

A Tapestry of Winter's Reverie

The world transforms, a canvas white,
Where animals don their gear, so tight.
A raccoon spins in a wild toboggan,
While owls wear mittens, oh, what a noggin!

Beneath the moon, they start a race,
Who knew the cold could prompt such grace?
A rabbit trips, a flurry of paws,
"Next time, I'll wear my fuzzy drawers!"

A frosty dance on frozen lakes,
With snowball fights and funny shakes.
Bunnies leap and try to dive,
Unicorns chuckle, feeling alive!

With cups of chocolate, they toast the night,
In this chilly world, everything's bright.
Laughter echoes, a sweet little tune,
In cozy nooks, beneath the moon!

Dreams Draped in Ivory Shrouds

The flurries dance with merry flair,
As bears sip cocoa without a care.
They stumble and fumble, such clumsy calls,
With marshmallows flying, oh, the balls!

A hidden treasure, a jolly sight,
An elf with snowballs, locked in a fight.
"Take that, ya' reindeer!" he boldly shouts,
While little kids cheer, laughing out loud!

Penguins slide to steal the show,
With funny hats, they'll surely glow.
In this chilly chaos, friends unite,
As snow plows rumble, what a delight!

Among the drifts, they dream away,
With playful spins, they greet the day.
In winter's bloom, they twist and twine,
A jolly crew, so divine!

Hushed Murmurs of the Cold

In winter's hush, whispers collide,
As fluffy friends begin to glide.
A squirrel cracks jokes atop a tree,
While ice skates twirl with glee and spree!

A bunny hops, but takes a fall,
They laugh so hard, the echoes call.
With goofy glances and cheeky grins,
They paint the landscape with wintry spins!

Chilly nights with garlands bright,
Where laughter bubbles, pure delight.
A bonfire crackling, tales unfold,
Of snowmen's antics and frosty bold!

So gather 'round this winter's cheer,
With giggles ringing, crystal clear.
For in this shivery, joyful night,
We celebrate fun, oh what a sight!

Celestial Flurry

Tiny dancers in the air,
Spinning 'round without a care.
They tickle noses, what a scene,
While dogs chase them, all routine!

Giggles burst with every fall,
As children slip, they have a ball.
With cheeks so red and laughter loud,
They make their parents oh so proud!

Fluffy hats and cozy mitts,
Creating art with clumsy wits.
A snowman's smile, a crooked grin,
Who's ready for a snowball win?

Then with a plop, the fun goes wild,
A splash lands on the unsuspecting child.
Laughter echoes, pure delight,
As winter's magic turns to light.

Slumbering Beneath the Ice

Underneath the chilly sheet,
A squirrel dreams of nuts to eat.
Waking briefly to complain,
He wonders where his stash has lain.

A penguin waddles, ice-bound knight,
Freezing toes in morning light.
He peers around—no fish in sight,
As snowflakes dance, oh what a fright!

Yet all is calm, the world asleep,
While fluffy critters play and leap.
They prance about, such goofy sights,
In puffy coats, hilarious nights!

Beneath the frost, a secret's kept,
Where dreams of summer dare to crept.
With slapstick moves, it's quite the show,
As frozen friends put on a glow!

Ethereal Drift

Floating down from up on high,
A fluffy peanut from the sky.
It lands upon a big, soft hat,
And giggles echo, 'What's up with that?'

A rabbit hops with fluffy flair,
Drawing circles in the air.
Who knew that winter could be grand,
With all these jokes made by the hand?

You might just trip and dance around,
Like a wobbly, jelly-bound mound.
Laughter spills with every slip,
As chocolate treats make hearts do flips!

A game of tag, the air is thick,
With icy giggles, all so quick.
And as they tumble in the snow,
The wonder blooms, in laughter's glow!

Serene Frost

In winter's hush, the world's a blank,
Where penguins throw a frosty prank.
A snowball fight breaks out with glee,
As snowmen cheer and sip some tea!

The icicles are trembling loud,
From laughter ringing through the crowd.
A dance-off starts next to the tree,
With wobbly moves—a sight to see!

Chubby cheeks and noses red,
While everyone hops out of bed.
A marshmallow fight takes soars and flies,
And giggles melt the frosty skies!

So in this chill, the joy runs deep,
While everyone is laughing, no time for sleep.
With fun and laughter as their craft,
The frozen world is full of craft!

Lachrymose Drifts

A snowball fight begins at dawn,
With laughter echoing, we all yawn.
My aim is true, or so I thought,
But missed my friend, who swiftly shot!

A frosty chill, a giggle spree,
They slipped and fell; oh, what a scene!
Wipe your face, it's not so bad,
But frozen pants? That's just plain mad!

Flakes flutter down like feathers in flight,
While whimsical snowmen take their bite.
One arm's a branch, the other a broom,
But his button eyes bring us all to gloom!

So let's embrace this chilly jest,
With warm hot cocoa, we're feeling blessed.
For in this white, our laughter drifts,
While frosty gleams send jolly gifts!

Whispers of Frosted Whimsy

In the blizzard, we're running fast,
With cheeks aglow, nothing can outlast!
Tip over here, a tumble there,
We laugh so hard, it's hard to bear!

The cat watches from its comfy chair,
While we make angels without a care.
"Is that a snowman or just my dad?"
With a carrot nose, we all go mad!

Gloves worn inside out, so silly indeed,
Slipping and sliding, oh, take heed!
Caught a snowball that wasn't meant,
Now it's my face that feels quite spent!

Yet as the sun begins to gleam,
We cherish this frosty, fun-filled dream.
With giggles and capers, the world is gay,
In this coldness, we'll frolic and play!

Crystal Kisses from the Sky

Watch the flakes fall, what a delight,
Each one a wish that takes to flight.
A dance so graceful, all askew,
Almost as funny as last night's stew!

We chase the cold until we freeze,
Then warm our hands among the peas!
A sledding race with awkward grace,
I'm pretty sure I lost my place!

Mittens mismatched, but who can tell?
As we tumble down, oh, what the hell!
A fort of dreams built tall and proud,
But now it's all a snowy shroud.

The gusts will carry a hearty cheer,
With icy giggles that we hold dear.
Here's to winter with all its charms,
A time for laughter, and cozy warms!

A Dance of Winter's Breath

With each new flake, a jig begins,
My hat spins round, disaster wins.
As I try to twirl and spin with glee,
I trip on ice, who knew it'd be?

Frosty breath like dragon fire,
We'll leap and skip, never tire!
Except for my friend who lost a sock,
Now more like an icicle on the block!

The winter's tune is wildly sweet,
With snow-covered boots, we dance on fleet.
A slide, a bump, and then a fall,
The neighbor's dog thinks it's a ball!

But in this frolic, warm hearts blend,
With silly snow games that will never end.
So let's spin out under the pale moonlight,
In this wondrous chill, our spirits take flight!

Mystic Blanket

A chilly night the world does freeze,
With fluffy white, it tickles knees.
Yet as I trudge, I slip and spin,
My bum goes down, and snow gets in!

The dogs they dance, they leap with cheer,
While I just grumble, mutter near.
A snowman winks, with carrot nose,
I swear he laughed as I fell, who knows?

A snowball flies, it hits my back,
I whirl around, it's joy, not lack.
Laughter echoes through the trees,
As snowmen giggle in the breeze!

So here I am in winter's glee,
Wrapped in fluff, I still can't see.
But with each fall, a grin expands,
In this white world, we share our plans!

Journey of Ice

On a frozen lake, I took a glide,
As graceful as a turkey, I tried to slide.
With each bold move, I lost my feet,
And landed hard, what a cold, cold treat!

Penguins passed, they pointed and swayed,
While I just laughed, I couldn't be dismayed.
Their waddle is art, they just don't care,
While I skated like I had two left pairs!

But lo! A snowman waved his stick,
I brought gifts of snowballs, hope they don't stick!
We laughed till we cried, what a sight,
As I learned that ice isn't all just fright!

So here I am, still on my quest,
To conquer the ice with all my zest.
Next time I'll bring, the fancy gear,
But till then, it's giggles and cheer!

Flickering Twilight

In evening's glow, with sparkles bright,
The moon brings chuckles; such silly flight!
A cat on a fence tries to take a leap,
But oops! Down it goes, oh what a heap!

Birds in sweaters, quite on parade,
Chirp winter songs, they're far from weighed.
Each flurry stirs up a quirky dance,
While I juggle mittens, oh what a chance!

Carrot noses roll past my shoe,
As I toss a snowball, what else to do?
They bounce and slip, like a comedic reel,
In this magical world, what a deal!

As stars emerge from the foggy sea,
I smile wide, so wild and free.
For in this twilight, we share our cheer,
With laughter and fun, what a night, my dear!

The Silence Between

Where whispers hide under blankets thick,
A snowman sneezes, I watch, quite a trick!
He tips his hat, though it's made of snow,
And laughs at me while the winds blow.

Icicles form, turning things to art,
What's majestic here… is a broken heart.
As I slip and fall, the cats look bemused,
They toast to the blessings that winter infused!

A raccoon in boots digs through the white,
Finding treasures in snow that shine, oh so bright!
"Hey!" I shout with a wink and a grin,
"Don't eat the snow if you know where you've been!"

So here we are, in laughter's embrace,
Each tumble, each slip, so full of grace.
Our wintery hearts, they dance and tease,
In this hush of joy, we find our ease!

Frozen Dances of Hope

In the chill, a jolly bear,
Twirls around without a care,
He slips and slides, does the jig,
Oh, look at that! A jumping pig!

With mittens worn on fluffy paws,
They spin like tops—what a cause!
A snowman stomps, a snowball flies,
Who knew these flakes could bring such highs?

While penguins waddle joyfully,
A party starts unintentionally,
The frosty breeze sings silly tunes,
As they dance beneath the moons.

With every hop and giggle shared,
Dreams of warmth still lightly bared,
In this fun, amidst the cold,
Jokes of thawing hearts unfold.

Whispers Beneath a Moonlit Veil

A snow cat whispers, oh so sly,
To a wide-eyed hare nearby,
"Can you catch a falling star?"
"I'll just stick to this frozen jar!"

They tickle icicles; laughter flies,
While watching fish that momentarily rise,
The winter night's a silly scheme,
Filled with giggles and pure esteem.

The wise old owl joins the fun,
Says, "Have you tried to catch the sun?"
With wings spread wide, he takes a leap,
Now that's a secret quiet to keep!

Each shadow dances, taking flight,
Chasing giggles through the night,
In a world so white and bright,
Whispers linger, pure delight.

Chasing Shadows in Frosted Light

A bear in shades, feeling quite bold,
Rides a sled—what a sight to behold!
He crashes down, a fluffy disgrace,
Rolling in snow with style and grace.

The shadows laugh, they leap with glee,
As rabbits hop around a tree,
They giggle as they stir the scene,
Playing pranks on all they glean.

Through frosted light, the whispers play,
As froggies croak the night away,
Dancing wildly on icy ground,
Turning silence into sound.

With twinkles bright, they skip and prance,
In this chilly, dreamy dance,
Even the moon can't help but grin,
At the silly chaos deep within.

Enigmas Wrapped in Crystal

The old tree speaks in a jolly riddle,
As squirrels play their merry fiddle,
"What's colder than a frozen heart?"
"The ice cream truck! Now that's an art!"

In crystal prisms, humor shines,
As kittens chase their snowy lines,
They tumble down with furry grace,
Laughter etched upon their face.

While snowdrops giggle, twirling spry,
A grid of giggles fills the sky,
Each flake a chuckle, small and light,
Creating wonders through the night.

The dance of mystery continues here,
In silly whispers for all to cheer,
An enigma wrapped in cheerful view,
Frosty fun that feels just like new.

Celestial Dreams Amongst the Chill

In the air, a dance of fluff,
Twirling around, not tough enough.
They land on noses, oh what a surprise,
Tickle the cheeks, bring laughter to eyes.

Whispers of frost, a giggle or two,
A slippery slide on a sparkly view.
Chasing the flakes, we run wild with glee,
Our hats blown off, like a cat in a tree.

Puffs on my tongue, melt without a care,
Like nibbling clouds, that float in the air.
We freeze in a pose, a frosty tableau,
And fall with a thud, an icy hello.

With every cold breath, our laughter can grow,
In a winter wonderland, put on a show.
While sipping hot chocolate, we cheerfully grin,
For the best kind of mischief has just begun!

Frostbitten Fantasies at Dusk

A flurry of giggles as darkness draws near,
Chasing the shadows, without any fear.
Breath foggy wisps, like cotton candy light,
We tumble and roll, oh what a delight!

With boots that are heavy and pants full of snow,
We leap like rock stars, as our laughter will flow.
A snowman is built, with a carrot for style,
But a snowball flies by—oh the humor's worthwhile!

Sleds racing down hills, with a whoosh and a laugh,
Flopping like fish, as we dance on the path.
The moon gives a wink, lighting up our fun,
Turning frostbitten mischief into great joy for everyone!

When the stars start to twinkle, we gather in glee,
Dreams of white wonders, as silly can be.
So let's spin in circles till we all fall around,
In this cold, silly world, where laughter is found!

A Blanket of Tranquil White

Under the covers, a soft padded dream,
Who knew that the flakes could giggle and gleam?
They pile up high; make a fluffy big mound,
And with every loud crunch, joy is unbound.

Dressed up like marshmallows, we bounce and we play,
With cheeks all aglow from our fun-filled ballet.
Snowball fights erupt in a flurry of cheer,
But careful, my friend, there's a penguin quite near!

When silence takes over, and stars fill the sky,
We hear all the whispers, oh my, oh my!
They giggle and chatter, these jesters of white,
Reviving our spirits on this cozy night.

So let's squeeze out the fun from this frosty delight,
With dreams made of laughter, and giggles that light.
For in the soft quiet, and in the pure play,
The joy of the winter will brighten our day!

Letters in the Frost

On window panes, they make their marks,
Like tiny dancers, in evening parks.
An O, an X, a wiggly D,
Who knew frost had such zest for glee?

They scribble tales of icy charm,
While in my mug, I sip warm balm.
"Dear friend," they say, "it's time to play!"
Until the sun wipes them away.

Giggling whispers on grassy beds,
To sledding hills and cozy spreads.
Each letter holds a secret cheer,
As winter giggles oh so near.

In playful hues, they swirl and twirl,
Chasing pine cones, making boys whurl.
With that first snow, they love to tease,
So come and join, if you please!

Whispering Winds of Winter

The breeze is up to something sly,
It tickles noses as it passes by.
Whispers of snowmen with silly hats,
And polar bears doing silly acrobats!

It carries jokes of slips and falls,
As mittens clatter against the walls.
A gusty giggle, oh what a sight,
As icicles dangle, sharp yet light.

Breath turns to fog, a playful plume,
Frosted gardens with a humorous bloom.
The trees may giggle with branches bending,
At how we stomp, as laughter's blending.

So listen close, the whispers blame,
For every snowball tossed is part of the game.
In winter's jest, we laugh and glide,
On frozen paths, we take our ride!

Dreams Wrapped in White

Crisp bites of air make cheeks like red,
Cozy dreams dance in our heads.
Pajamas tussled, a pillow fight,
While outside, the world is clothed in white.

Under blankets, we giggle low,
As the snowman starts to grow and grow.
With carrots for noses, no plans to fight,
He waves a stick arm, oh what a sight!

While chilly winds hum their frosty song,
The laughter carries, it won't be long.
With every snowball and playful scream,
We build our stories, wrapped in cream.

Cocoa mugs ready, with marshmallows bright,
As evening falls and brings the night.
In this soft world, let's always play,
With laughter echoing throughout the day!

The Palette of Cold

A canvas stretched o'er the town's domain,
With frigid fingers, it cracks in vain.
The sky spills color, a splash of fun,
With icy blues, till day is done.

Painted rooftops, like frosting sweet,
While children sneak on laughter's beat.
They paint with snowballs, easy and free,
Creating art for all to see!

Pick of the mix, a sled on the hill,
With giggles booming, a joyful thrill.
Each brush of cold brings smiles, they reign,
'Til mischievous sunshine melts it away again.

So let us splash and let us play,
In the palette of cold, we find our way.
For winter's charm brings joy anew,
In a canvas bright, where dreams come true!

Chasing Stardust in the Cold

In winter's air, a giggle floats,
A dance of cold on fluffy coats.
Around we spin, like crazy mice,
While shovels wait, our hearts entice.

The sky is dark, like chocolate charm,
Yet here we are, a growing swarm.
With cups of cocoa, cheers abound,
As flurries tumble to the ground.

A snowball fight, a slippery laugh,
In this winter game, we're all a gaffe.
The neighbors peek, their grins exposed,
As laughter echoes, we all doze.

So here we chase that twinkling gleam,
In frosty bliss, we live our dream.
With every slip and every slide,
We paint the cold with joy and pride.

Moonlit Silence

Under the moon, the world's aglow,
We waddle like ducks in boots of snow.
With icy noses and eyes so bright,
We craft our castles in the night.

The quiet falls, yet giggles soar,
As tongues stick out, we yell for more.
With wild jumps and silly sounds,
We're kings and queens of snowy grounds.

A snowman springs with a crooked grin,
Sporting a hat as thick as skin.
With carrot noses, we shake our heads,
And laugh at tales that fill our beds.

So in this world of white and cheer,
We find our joy, year after year.
Embracing freeze with warm delight,
As winter giggles take their flight.

Winter's Gentle Embrace

The blanket falls, so soft, so white,
We tumble down, what a funny sight!
With puffy coats and hats askew,
We wave at snowmen passing through.

The trees wear coats of icy lace,
While frosty breath paints every face.
We roll about, we leap and bound,
As laughter drifts with frosty sound.

Caught in a flurry, we spin around,
Throwing our arms like we've just found,
A treasure chest of giggling dreams,
In winter's hug, life's more than it seems.

With flapping mittens, we start to race,
In this chilly maze, we find our place.
Joy's in the air, as shadows play,
In winter's arms, we laugh and sway.

Soft Lullabies of Snow

As flakes descend like feathery cheer,
We make our wishes, our hopes sincere.
With every drop, a story starts,
As playful whispers fill our hearts.

A quiet hum of laughter's tune,
While snowmen dance beneath the moon.
With rosy cheeks and playful ears,
We spin round, dissolving fears.

In every shoveled path we trace,
We leave our mark, a jolly space.
With cocoa dreams and marshmallow poise,
We're wrapped in love, we're filled with noise.

Oh, how we twirl in fluffy gowns,
In winter fun, we wear our crowns.
So let the night with laughter glow,
As we embrace the soft, sweet flow.

Ephemeral Chill

In winter's grasp, we bundle tight,
With scarves so big, we lose our sight.
We trip on ice, a clumsy dance,
As penguins laugh, we take a chance.

Hot cocoa spills upon our clothes,
The marshmallows stick like tiny foes.
We giggle as we shiver through,
Pretending it's a trendy brew.

The frostbite nips our rosy cheeks,
But in the snow, it's fun that speaks.
A snowball fight, we launch with glee,
Who knew that winter could be free?

And when we slip upon our tails,
The hoots and howls, like winter's gales.
Though winter isn't always sweet,
It's filled with laughs, not cold defeat.

Frost-Kissed Fantasies

A rabbit hops in boots too big,
He tries to dance, but oh, the jig!
He leaps and trips, a sight to see,
While squirrels cheer with wild decree.

A snowman wears a floppy hat,
He can't find hands, just a ski chat.
The carrot nose begins to droop,
As everyone joins the icy troop.

The flakes descend, they twirl and whirl,
Like tiny jewels, they jump and swirl.
We catch them on our tongues with flair,
And laugh at how they muss our hair.

As icicles hang like glittered dew,
We make a wish, while sipping brew.
In frosty times, we find delight,
With giggles born from winter's bite.

Hushed Winter Serenade

In the quiet, we hear a sneeze,
A bear wakes up, "Oh, where's my cheese?"
He searches high and low with dread,
While birds just chirp, "Please go to bed!"

The snow drifts soft on sleepy trees,
A bunny hops, "Hey, snatch my peas!"
But every bite, he drops in fright,
As snowflakes tickle, what a sight!

The sky's a dream in shades of gray,
Where angels dance and squirrels play.
With every puff of frosty breath,
We try to hide, but it's a mess!

With melted hats and soggy gloves,
The laughter floats like skies above.
Though winter wraps in chilly seams,
We find our joy in muffled dreams.

Beyond the Winter's Blanket

A woolly sheep spins tales of fun,
Of frosty fields and warm sunshine.
He grins and leaps, then finds a way,
To sneak a nap on snowy play.

The children race, oh what a sight,
Slipping here and sliding right.
They tumble down with squeals so loud,
Creating laughter, large and proud.

A cat in mittens struts with glee,
Pretending it's the place to be.
She swipes at flakes with tiny paws,
Proclaiming winter's greatest flaws.

And when the night draws stars so bright,
We cozy up, hearts filled with light.
For while it's cold and chilly too,
The warmth within will see us through.